YOU CAN
MAKE IT

The Power of Choices

Nazaire Rutledge

Copyright 2019 by Nazaire Rutledge

All rights reserved

No part of this publication may be reproduced, stored in a retrieval system or transmitted in any way by any means, electronic, photocopy, recording or otherwise without the prior permission of the author except as provided by USA copyright law.

This novel is a work of fiction. Names, descriptions, entities, and incidents included in the story are products of the author's imagination. Any resemblance to actual persons, events and entities is entirely coincidental.

Table of Contents

Dedication 1
Acknowledgements 2
Foreword 5
Introduction 8
The Beginning 11
Life without a Father 17
Motherless and Traumatized 27
Music State of Mind 33
Saved by Grace 41
The Promise 47
Plot Change 55
Strength and Restoration 61
Guidance for the Journey 69
The Author 74

Dedication

This book is dedicated to my brother Da'mique, my nephew Kingston, and every Black male in America. Your life matters and becomes the sum total of the choices you make.

Acknowledgements

Proverbs 3:6 commands us to acknowledge God in all our ways so I honor Him first. He has been exceptional to me all of my life. It is because of His unconditional love and favor that I am still here today. It may sound cliche,' but I honestly do not know where I would be if it had not been for the Lord on my side.

A special thank you to my fiancé,' Danielle. You are my best friend and my biggest supporter. You pushed me to make my dream come true despite the many times I wanted to quit and leave this story in my notes. You are God's gift to me and I am eternally grateful for you. I love you.

To my Grandma, I love you girl! You are and will forever be one of the greatest blessings that God gave me.

To my pastor and father figure, Dr. Lorenzo Smalls, Sr. Thank you for praying with and for me. I do not have adequate words to express my gratitude for the spiritual insight and confirmation you provided to help me put this story out.

To my professor, Dr. Bagasra, thank you for writing such a captivating and inspiring foreword. I knew that you could do it! You have been such a great support to me since my freshman year in college and I am most appreciative!

To my publishing company, thank you all so much for everything. You guys were such great assistance and helped me make this dream a reality. I can never repay you for what you have done.

To all of my other supporters, family, and friends, I appreciate you all immensely. Thank you for believing in me.

May God continue to bless you all. Stay tuned for part II.

Foreword

Nazaire Rutledge is a 2019 graduate of Claflin University with a Bachelor's Degree in Psychology and a minor in Sociology. As a student in my psychology courses a few years ago, he may have heard the following quote from Victor Frankl, an existential psychologist and holocaust survivor who wrote in his best-selling book *Man's Search for Meaning*: "*Everything can be taken from a man but one thing: the last of the human freedoms — to choose one's attitude in any given set of circumstances, to choose one's own way.*" Nazaire embodies this quote in his own life, as he chooses to maintain a positive attitude and outlook no matter the circumstances. This book is a testimony to both the power of trauma and the ultimate triumph of resiliency.

Nazaire's story and advice speak to the great desire of many young Black men who wish to break generational curses through education, observation, self-reflection, and forgiveness. If we take control of our own destiny by acknowledging our past and working towards a better future, we can achieve anything. This is certainly evidenced in this book.

Often in psychology we talk about trauma, especially the traumas of childhood which are now referred to as adverse childhood experiences (ACEs). We see a lot of research on the negative impact of ACEs on physical and mental health outcomes in adulthood. We also see a lot of research on the impact of socioeconomic status, poor education systems, and other environmental factors on future success. What is lacking in contemporary psychological and sociological research is the testimonies of young men like Nazaire, whose lived experiences reflect such statistics, and yet their realities also reflect that they have overcome the many adversities placed before them to not just survive but also thrive. Our environments and our past are not chains that cannot be broken.

I knew a little of Naz's story when he was a student, and I am pleased to see that he has put his experiences and thoughts together to share with others. It is his voice, and the voices of others like him that we need the most in these challenging times.

Anisah Bagasra, PhD

Assistant Professor of Psychology

Kennesaw State University

Introduction

▲▲▲▲▲▲▲▲▲▲▲▲

The decision to write a book is not an easy one. And if I'm honest, I certainly did not want to write this one because I was so worried about what people would think about me as they learned about my past. But after consulting God and some of the authentic people in my life, I realized that I needed to share my experience. Why? The help my story can potentially offer not just me, but the world, is indescribable. To not do so would be - selfish. I realize now more than ever that in order to fully live, we must embrace our past.

I warn you. This is the raw, authentic, and uncut story of Nazaire - with some thoughtfulness given to protecting my family. The events you will read about broke me down, but they are also the ones that built me into the man I am today. I share it to encourage those individuals who feel like they cannot make it - either because of their past or their current situations. At the end of every section, you will find encouragement and positive messages coupled with a life lesson from my personal experience. I challenge you to apply them to your life as you deem appropriate.

We all have a story and the freedom to choose what we will do with it. As the author of my story, I have chosen to be transparent. I have chosen to make a difference by sharing my story in hopes of motivating those with a similar story. By no means have I arrived. I am working my way through the struggle to express my innermost feelings, and each day I get a step closer to my healing. I hope this book will help others do the same.

The Beginning

▲▲▲▲▲▲▲▲▲▲▲▲

In 1906 Jennie Wilson wrote a song entitled, *"Hold to God's Unchanging Hand."* In the first verse of the song are the words, "Time is filled with swift transition," and those six words describe my life perfectly. I had to very quickly learn how to hold to God's hand. As you read through this book it will become abundantly clear as to you why.

I was born Thursday July 17, 1997 to Crystal Session and the late Elton N. Rutledge Jr. I was not born with a silver spoon in my mouth nor did I get everything that I wanted, but I had love, shelter, food, protection, and God's favor. I grew up in the city limits of Georgetown, SC - where you know you are home when you smell the stench of the mill and see the infamous hustlers begging on the streets.

To many, Georgetown is known for its historic downtown waterfront, high tourist activity, and great seafood. For me, however, Georgetown is a place where many possess potential but grapple with complacency. Town, as I call it, is not all bad but does have high crime rates, low-income families, few job opportunities, racism, and an overall lack of support for one another. Where I grew up there were inadequate resources for struggling families, transportation barriers, continuous drug activity, and active violence. I was ashamed of my environment and living conditions, and hated bringing my friends around who lived better than I did. We lived in an out-dated mobile home while they lived in two story homes. While I appreciated what we had, I did not appreciate the struggle. I just didn't get it.

Rather than being consumed by lack and strife, I chose to embrace my life - because it was mine. I knew at a young age, however, that I did not want to live that way all my life. My environment lit a fire inside of me. I was determined to succeed in life so I could help my family *"get out,"* and experience better opportunities. My circumstances birthed a sense of resilience in me, and reinforced the fact that it is not about what happens to you, but how you respond to it that really matters. I learned a few lessons - survival, to go after what I want with or without support from others, and that nothing comes free.

Growing up, people often referred to me as *"grandma's bo*y*"* because she raised me. For years I denied it, but as I grew older I had to admit that it was true. I did not mind it at all because grandma is the epitome of love. If you know me then you know that I love her something serious. She unselfishly raised me and my siblings, and provided for us in a way that was incomparable. For as long as I can remember, my grandmother simply made it happen. There was *never* a time that we went without the basic necessities. I sometimes reflect back and wonder how we made it, but then I am reminded of the many sacrifices my grandmother made to ensure that my sisters and I were good. After raising her three children, she took on the responsibility of raising five more. She could have easily allowed us to go astray or stay in the predicament we were in, but she did not. I will give her the world for that very reason.

Grandma was not perfect, but she gave her all in everything she did for us. Most importantly, the life that she lived in front of me helped me find Jesus, taught me how to *survive*, and ultimately helped mold me into the man I am today. In my twenty plus years on this earth, there has not been one thing that I asked my grandma for that she did not provide. I often say that if someone ever searched for the definition of sacrifice, my grandmother's picture has to be right there. I am forever grateful for her and her unconditional love. Despite the love, sacrifices and mothering from my grandmother, I still often felt like a motherless child because I did not live with my biological mother. That brought a lot of emotions with it because in all honesty, I wanted to be with my mother.

At an early age, my grandmother instilled in me the importance of God and church. I joined First Calvary Missionary Baptist Church under the leadership of Dr. Lorenzo Smalls, Sr. We initially started attending the 7 AM service, but that was not enough for me. I also started attending the 11 AM service with my aunts, Verdell and Mary. I loved church so much that if my grandmother or aunts did not go, I would cry then settle for listening to it on the radio. Eventually I started singing in the choir and serving on several committees, so I started walking to church by myself. I grew such a love for the church and for God that I did not miss a Sunday. I also began hanging out with my Pastor's grandson and eventually spent the night. I yearned for time with males, and wanted to be at the church and under my Pastor all the time.

You would think that being in church all your life and having so many pathways to God would exempt you from certain things. My perception was wrong and the reality is that my life was *hell*. Church was the mask I used to hide my honest sentiments about what I was going through at home. I was under the impression that if I stayed in church under my pastor, my misery and confusion would disappear and my life would miraculously get better. But, I was sadly mistaken. The process to my healing would require much more than just attending church, but I was too young to know that.

Life Lesson:

Sometimes we wear masks or throw ourselves into church, work or some other situation to survive. Be encouraged and know that you do not have to settle for that. It is an exhausting lifestyle. Embrace the real you and do the hard work required to be whole.

Life Without A Father

▲▲▲▲▲▲▲▲▲▲▲▲

I loved my dad immensely and I loved being with him. He was a consistent presence in my life and we shared some fond memories. I loved our walks to the barbershop to get my haircut and going to visit my cousin Corey's house. I also remember when my father was incarcerated, my mom would take me and my sister to go visit him. I loved how every time we would go, my dad would buy me a Tahitian Treat drink. My fondest memory overall is the day we walked down Prince Street to my Auntie Lena Mae's house and she took a picture of us - the only picture I have with my father.

I can still recall being with my dad earlier that day - August 3, 2002. I remember him telling me he had somewhere to go, but he would be back. When it reached a certain time of the day and he was not back, I got upset. I kept asking my mother and my grandma when my dad would come back for me like he promised. They did not have an answer. Eventually I started seeing the faces of my dad and his friend pop up on the news. I thought he was famous since he was on TV, but I was too young to read the headline - "MISSING." I had no idea that I would never see him again.

Sadly, on that fateful day my father and his friend died a horrific death, and I was not prepared for it. I cannot even put into words what I felt when I heard news. I felt distraught, my heart ached, and it seemed that I would never fully heal. Looking back now, I believe God placed it on my Auntie Lena Mae's heart to take the picture of us the day we walked to her house. God knew that He would soon take him from me. I do not remember many conversations with my dad, but I do remember him telling me that he was coming back. He hugged me and my sister, and told us that he loved us before he left.

The man accused of shooting my father, and his accomplice, claim to this day that they did not do it. However, there are witnesses and statements contradicting their story. Several people allege that he told them he shot two men because they cheated him out of drug money. Those allegations are contradicted by a statement that a convicted serial killer paid my father and his friend to kill the murderer. There are even stories about them moving the remains more than once to keep vultures away and the police from discovering their remains.

Law enforcement and detectives worked diligently to locate the remains, and everyday I would ask the Lord to please bring my daddy home. At five years old I had faith that my prayer would be answered, but obviously God had another plan. After about two weeks the remains of my father and his friend were found in a burlap bag dumped off in a swampy wooded area. I still cannot come to grips with why someone would do something so cruel. Regardless of the situation, they did not deserve that and neither did their families.

I still remember the day of his funeral - the procession, my cousin singing, "*What God has for me it is for me*," and my grandfather going from the first row to the pulpit to preach his son's eulogy. The part that I recall most vividly is when we got to the cemetery and my cousin lifted me up to place a card on my dad's casket before it was lowered in the ground. That memory often replays in my mind.

For years, I had dreams and mental flashbacks about everything that occurred during that time in my life. The inability to get such tragic memories out of my head was a signal that I needed help to effectively deal with it. I could not do it though because I did not know how. I just wish my father's remains had been found sooner so I could have seen him one more time for closure.

With my dad gone, I decided at a young age that I would help my grandmother raise my sisters. I devoted myself to being a positive male figure in their lives. Unfortunately, I was so focused on being who and what they needed that for years I ignored the trauma and adverse impact of it all on me. I was completely oblivious to the damage it was wreaking in my life, and never publicly expressed my sentiments until now.

Life without a father has been difficult, and while I never lacked, there was a hole in my heart for a very long time. I desperately want to share many important events in my life with my father. God had other plans, but I honestly did not agree with His plan. In fact, I hated it and I was angry with God. I had many pent-up and mixed emotions about my father's death. I envied my friends and classmates who were blessed to have their fathers in their lives. For years I struggled to manage the jealousy, but it ultimately encompassed my thoughts, feelings, and behaviors, and manifested as anger. My peers did not do anything to me and it was not their fault that my father was killed. I knew that in my heart, but because they had something I wanted but could not have, they subconsciously became a threat in my mind. I hurt badly and had no idea how to fix it.

Typically, when a tragedy of this magnitude strikes children have the support of family, but my sister and I were not fortunate enough to receive full support from my dad's family. A select few stuck by us while the others stopped claiming us. I longed for a relationship with my paternal grandparents. They were the closest part of my dad that I had left, but they did not want any dealings with me or my sister. I really could not understand why. When my father was alive and I visited them, they loved on me the way grandparents should. On the other hand, when I went there alone my aunts would torture me. They would hang me up on a nail on the bedroom door and leave me there for hours. There were times I hung there so long that I used the bathroom on myself. Even though I screamed and cried, no one came to my rescue until my grandfather came home and took me down. I am convinced that it was only because they did not believe I was really their nephew. As sad as this may sound, the only relief I had from my father's death was the fact that I no longer had to visit and deal with the torture.

Until October 14, 2014, I was convinced that they all hated me. That day, for whatever reason, my grandfather messaged me on Facebook and stated three words that resonate in my mind even to this day. He said, "You are loved." It was the first time I had spoken with him in quite a while, and it reassured me about a lot of things. I had planned on inviting him to my high school graduation in hopes that we could mend our relationship, but on January 11, 2015 - just four months before my graduation, he died after a brief illness. I had mixed emotions because I knew my intentions, but I had to accept what God allowed. I will never forget how I felt when I read the direct message I received from my cousin - while at church - letting me know that he had passed away.

To be close to him even in death, I devised a plan. I rushed home from church then walked from home to the hospital to meet my co-worker from the funeral home. He had been called to pick up the remains, but had no idea that it was my grandfather. When he found out, he was concerned and asked if I was sure I wanted to do it. I assured him that I did, knowing it was likely the only way I would get close. When I walked in the ICU and saw him lying there lifeless, I just wanted it to all be a dream.

Unfortunately, it wasn't and that day changed my life forever. Years later, however, I learned from my aunt that he would talk about me and my sister often. She said he really wanted to see us and be a part of our lives, but did not want us to be mistreated. That spoke volumes to me.

As if the hurt of his passing was not enough, I had the unfortunate experience of seeing my paternal grandmother at a funeral in December 2017. When she saw me, she sat down beside me - not to make amends - but to ask me if I would take a DNA test to determine if I was actually family. She and her daughters still did not believe that I was my father's son. I could not believe that at age 20 and 15 years after my father's demise, she would approach me with such a request. All I could think was, *"How dare she?!"* She told me there were rumors that someone else was my dad, but that she still loved me like her own regardless. Her actions actually said the opposite to me so I refused to do it. I have nothing to prove to anyone. My father knew he had three kids before he was killed, and that is all that matters.

As I continue to grow older and experience life, I still sometimes long for a relationship with both sides of my family. It is generally the same faithful few on my father's side who reach out and keep up with me. But despite what I want, I am learning to appreciate what I have. Life gets a little tough at times, but I choose to embrace what is and release what was. It is hard to believe that wanting a relationship with family can be so painful. In spite of it all, I know that God makes no mistakes, so I trust Him to use my experience for my good and His Glory. I am determined that when I become a father, I will be the best one I can to my kids. I will make sure that I am there through it all because I know how it feels to be without one.

I appreciate the men who stood in the gap to make sure I was good. People like my Pastor, Big Quentin, Travis, Desmond, Shawn, and Rev. Canteen, to name a few. They all saw what I was lacking, and they willingly and whole-heartedly offered me authentic, spiritual guidance.

Life Lesson:

Death is hard, in general, but to lose a parent is a blow that is indescribable. If your parents are still living, please do not take them for granted. There is someone wishing and praying they still had theirs. In addition, make sure that you know who you are and whose you are, and never lose sight of that. Sometimes life's distractions can be your own flesh and blood but even in that, you must be confident and steadfast.

Motherless and Traumatized

▲▲▲▲▲▲▲▲▲▲▲▲

I still have memories of my early childhood, and the good times we had. My mom was the ideal mother. She worked hard, sacrificed a lot, and did everything for us. In fact, her world revolved around me and my sisters. Being raised predominately by a woman taught me some really good lessons. Soon, however, things began to change and we were exposed to a lot of negativity that left me feeling like I had not only lost my dad - but my mom, too.

As a young boy, I began to see men physically, mentally, and/or emotionally abusing almost every female who played a key role in my rearing. Sometimes the abuser was a man in my family and other times, it was a female in the family who was the victim. By about age 8 I had become so acquainted with abuse I thought it was the norm. Despite those thoughts, however, there was something deep down inside my heart compelling me to be different. I knew I could not be like my maternal grandfather nor my mother's paramour who most exposed me to abuse. I wanted desperately to be a different kind of man, but just did not know how.

I was perplexed by the fact that a man would beat a woman, curse her out, degrade her character, and scandalize her name. I began to question if the ideas I had about what a real man should be like were wrong. Instead of positive role models I saw doggish attributes. There just appeared to be a generational curse over my family, and I saw firsthand how it impacted my loved ones. Simply put, in my family it seemed that love was synonymous with pain.

For years I watched my mother's boyfriend abuse her, and it seemed to leave her with an unhealthy view of herself. He would spit on her, pull her hair, burn her, and shoot her with his bebe gun. He would also regularly lock her in the room away from us and verbally abuse her. The way he controlled her was disheartening and to make matters worse, I was too young to help her. In the beginning he seemed like a good guy, but the truth is he was really evil. He was an incompetent, conniving, hateful, and a manipulative individual who took her money, screwed up her name, diminished her credit, and isolated her from family and friends. We bounced back and forth between family as her craving for validation from him brainwashed her - ultimately to the point that she literally turned her back on her children. At about 10 years old I permanently moved in with my grandmother because he had started hitting on me and I got tired of seeing my mom go through that.

Grandma had tried to warn her, and would remind her that the door was always open for her to come home, but she did not. She thought my grandmother was being unsupportive and jealous, but she was really trying to protect her because she knew what it was like. Ignoring the warnings led her to a life plagued by domestic violence. As I see it, my mother was naïve and her boyfriend took advantage of that.

Witnessing domestic violence took me on an emotional rollercoaster. According to *americanfamilyphysican.org*, it is estimated that 3.2 million children witness incidents of domestic violence annually which leads to an array of negative cognitive, behavioral and emotional effects. Sadly, my siblings and I were a part of those statistics and all suffered individually from the negative effects of domestic violence. According to *brookings.edu*, males who are raised by single females, without fathers or consistent male mentors, are likely to fare worse on a number of dimensions including, social and emotional development and academic achievement. They are at greater risk of abuse from live-in boyfriends who are not their fathers and they may also develop a level of aggression that leads to general acts of violence. This is primarily because their lack has caused dysfunction and trauma they do not know how to address.

On the other hand, there is so much literature about the role of a father in the life of his daughter, and when he is not present, that void is felt. I did not want my sisters to feel the impact of their dad's absence so I had to step up. I had to become a void filler for them. I wanted them to love themselves first and then to feel the love of a man who wanted nothing from them in return. As their brother I was determined to be that. I wanted them to have self-respect and maintain high self-esteem so I had to model the characteristics of a gentleman. Finally, I wanted them to see what resilience looked like so I had to let my sisters see me have the courage to bounce back and take risks in the face of setbacks.

I searched hard to understand what led to such toxicity in my mother's life and why she allowed it to go on so long. Now I better understand what she was going through, and how hard it was to get out of such a toxic relationship. As a child, however, I did not and it caused me to build up a wall of hatred for her. Yes, I hated my own mother! I thought the void it created in my heart would never be filled. For years I legitimately felt like a motherless child, but in 2018 I was able to tear down the wall and fully forgive her. I was determined not to allow the grudges I had been holding to stop my growth. I just could not allow myself to be like her boyfriend or any other abusive man I had known.

Life Lesson:

Forgiveness is essential if you want to reach success or just live at peace. As hard as it may be to let grudges, hatred and pain go, it is necessary. When we do not release them, we are granting those things access into our minds and lives - where they do not deserve space. Domestic violence is real and the effects are harmful. If you or someone you know is affected by domestic violence, call 1-800-799-7233 for help.

Music State of
Mind

▲▲▲▲▲▲▲▲▲▲▲▲

Music has been an important part of my life for a very long time. From singing on the youth choir at my church to becoming a musician, music has played a pivotal role in making me who I am today. At first I did not think much of it, but now that I am older I realize just how powerful music is. I've seen people who are disabled respond to music in a way that is astounding. I have literally watched moods change by a simple phrase from a song. Music has a profound effect on my life and it has taught me lessons that still encourage me today. This quote by

Modest Mouse quite adequately sums it up, *"Music is to the soul what words are to the mind."*

My musical journey began with me singing on the youth choir at my church, and I thoroughly enjoyed it. People would tell me that I had a gift and that I would make it big, but I never saw what they did. I simply enjoyed singing. Clearly people other than my church members saw something in me because I was later drafted by my elementary school chorus teacher to join a group called The B.E.A.C.H. Singers. This was a large group of gifted and talented students from every school in the district and we traveled to sing. While I enjoyed singing on both choirs, I was always intrigued by the music behind the lyrics. Whether it was in church singing a Kirk Franklin song, in B.E.A.C.H. performing a song by Andrea Bocelli, or singing with my high school gospel choir, I *loved* the music. The feeling that the drums and the organ gave me in church seemed to penetrate my very soul, so I joined the drum line. That did not appease me like the organ and keyboard did though. While my church praised my voice, I wanted to both sing and play. I started to find myself in the musicians' pit after church and was sometimes more into the chord progressions being played than in singing. I would ask the organist a lot of questions in an attempt to learn as much as I could, but it still wasn't enough. So, I decided to teach myself.

I was eventually blessed with my first keyboard, and I used that and YouTube to teach myself how to play. I learned all the songs that my church sang frequently and even some patterns to just play freely. After some months of observing others, watching videos, and practicing, I was ready to make my debut. My pastor allowed me to play at his pastoral anniversary, but I did a *terrible* job. I mean it was horrific. It felt like a set-up. They sang all the songs that I practiced, but they did not go well. I was already hurt and extremely devastated, but church members made it even worse as several of them came up to me afterwards and told me to stick to singing. They did not hold back on telling me that I could not play. Man, I went home and cried my eyes out. No matter how much my grandma and pastor tried to encourage me, my self esteem was shot. Not only did I do a terrible job playing, but the "church folk" discouraged the hell out of me. I must be honest. I did not expect that kind of treatment from people in the church. I was mentally immature and expected that everyone would support me. That experience taught me that not everyone in the church had a heart of compassion like Christ.

As much as I wanted to give up after that experience, I just could not. Somehow I summoned the strength to keep going. I used those negative comments as motivation and surrounded myself with people who would help me as well as hold me accountable. It was not easy, but it turned out to be worth it. I was not satisfied with where I was musically and desperately wanted to improve. The first church that saw that and opened its doors to me was Elder Woodrow Nesbit and the Overflow Apostolic Church. The pastor and his sons were musicians who, for months, invested time to help me build my confidence and enhance my skills. Eventually I improved and was blessed with my first full time gig making $80 a Sunday. Everything fell into place with that church. They picked me up for rehearsal and church, fed me every Sunday, and paid me. I thought that I would be there my entire life, but God elevated me. That tenure came to an end and without me even looking, a pastor approached me at the end of a concert and asked me if I was playing for a church. When I replied "no," he offered me $150 a Sunday and agreed to pick me up for both rehearsal and Sunday morning service. They treated me very well and I stayed at that church and a few others until I graduated high school. This story is a testament to how small beginnings can humble us and open doors for us if we do not quit. Here I am six years later having had the opportunity to play for about nine churches and several gospel artists and groups, and I am currently in a position where my gift allows me to be compensated whatever I ask.

It was not easy and I am still learning daily, but I do not regret my musical journey at all. There were definitely times when I felt insignificant compared to my homeboys and other minstrels, but I realized that there was enough grind for everyone. We were all able to be impactful using our own uniqueness. The down times and mishaps pushed me along with people like Jessie Wilson, Lewis Morant, William and Antwan Dunmore, Kewaun Myers, Samuel Fulmore, Jarvis Jett, and Cameron Donalson to name a few. These boys urged me to keep trying until I reach my full potential. When I wanted to give up they would not, and still do not, let me. Instead they held me accountable and made me stay at the piano until I played the song correctly. While it may have taken a lot of embarrassment, long nights, tears, and prayers to be where I am, I am humbled by this journey and will always be grateful for it. It will never be about the checks, who I have played or will play for, neither will it matter how good I played. What will matter in the end is what I did with the gift God gave me. He gives the gift and what we do with it is our gift back to him. This phase of my life was so beneficial. It taught me the importance of growth, endurance and tenacity. It taught me how to keep progressing despite negativity. There have been many times when I had to turn to music for healing, peace of mind, or just simple encouragement. Over the years, I have learned to appreciate all genres of music. As I looked beyond just the musician realm, I began to see just how powerful music really is. That made me even more grateful that I did not give up on music.

Life Lesson:

Do it! Whatever it is that gives you a sense of drive, excitement, and passion. Keep hope alive and make it happen. *"The best way to not feel hopeless is to get up and do something. Don't wait for good things to happen to you. If you go out and make some good things happen, you will fill the world with hope, you will fill yourself with hope."*

~President Barack Obama

Saved by Grace

▲▲▲▲▲▲▲▲▲▲▲▲

Benjamin B. Warfield stated, *"Grace is free sovereign favor to the ill-deserving."* If I had to use three words to describe what the outcome of my life has been thus far it would be: "SAVED by GRACE." I was headed down the wrong path and although I knew that I was different, I desperately wanted to be like the people I hung around daily. I found myself doing stupid and dangerous things, and started losing sight of who I really was. I knew what I was doing was not right, and could see that God was still looking out for me. Every time my friends were about to do something against the law I always had church, choir rehearsal, or some type of side hustle that saved me from being a part of it. I did not judge my friends for their actions then or now. If it was not for the grace of God and the prayers of those covering me, I would have chosen the same path.

Fortunately, two long-term opportunities were presented to me while I was in the midst of my *"identity crisis,"* - a side job with a retired plumber and a part-time job at the funeral home. Thinking back on it now, I believe these opportunities were God's way of saving me and preserving my destiny. It is imperative to know that your destiny is determined by your decisions. Sometimes the changes of life can cause us to lose ourselves and make the wrong moves. As a result we lose focus and begin to go down the wrong path. It is then that God steps in, redirects, and safeguards our destiny in the meantime until we regain focus. I am convinced that is what He did for me.

On June 29, 2013, I started working at Wilds Funeral Home. I initially started coming around because I wanted full details on what my father's remains consisted of when they finally found him. But, once I got that information I wanted to learn more about the industry. It has always been a passion of mine to help everyone else around me, and this job gave me that opportunity. I grew a deep love for the funeral home and once my boss saw that, he offered me a job. Since starting I have not only learned about the industry and the history of

Wilds, but I had time to network and build relationships with other funeral homes, churches, and families and businesses in Georgetown and surrounding areas. I became well-known because of the exposure Wilds gave me.

The job came into my life at the right time, but I did not even realize it at first. My boss, Mel, eventually became my mentor and a consistent father figure. I needed that and the things I have learned from him are immeasurable. His involvement in my life proved to me that God had not forgotten about me. With his guidance, I learned the importance of creating a plan for my life, saving money, and sticking to my plan no matter what. He pushed me really hard to reach my full potential, and his lessons ultimately made me a better man in both life and business. In addition, the guidance that I received from my co-workers at Wilds, especially the late Mr. Marion Bessellieu, was ineffable. Mr. Bez, as we called him, was the GOAT. He taught me everything I know about the funeral home, including how to pick up the bodies, work the casket key, and effectively serve grieving families with care. He even secretly let me drive the hearse so I would know how to do it. Mr. Bez is the one who took me to buy my first car. He gave me the old school, but truthful tips to succeeding as a Black man. I will cherish him and everything he taught me until the day I die. It is really an amazing privilege to be attached to people who genuinely care and want the best for you.

During my time at Wilds, I also began working with a retired plumber named Elias Stewart, Jr. He literally taught me everything he knew about plumbing, and gave me valuable advice and tips that I still use today. Just by accepting the opportunities God placed in my life, I was able to remove myself from the company of individuals who meant me no good and learn how to love them from a distance. I went from smoking marijuana, vandalizing buildings and cars, stealing, lying, and so much more to buying my first car cash, and becoming the first in my immediate family to graduate high school and college. Everything that I went through during that time reminded me of God's grace and favor over my life, even though I did not deserve it given my track record. He sent me consistent people that He knew would help me get on track, fulfill my destiny, and again - hold me accountable. These guys probably have no idea how significant they are, but i dare not write this book without acknowledging the people who really saved me from losing myself, failing at life, jail time, and even possibly death.

I must be transparent and admit that there were several times during this *grace* phase where I felt bad about separating myself from my friends. Even though I was thankful for the help God gave me, I felt like I somewhat neglected them. They thought that I was trying to act like I was better than them, but that wasn't the case all. I had to grow up and learn to embrace my individuality, while accepting others for who and where they were. It was hard to accept the fact that I could not change people. We can each influence others, but the decision to change is an individual one. I had to accept the fact that we might not all have the same level of motivation, and even if we did - it might be about different things. We each have to fulfill our own life purpose. Everybody comes into your life for a reason. It is our job to determine what we will do with the lessons those individuals teach us. I decided to remain cordial, love from a distance and pursue my dreams with focus.

Life Lesson:

Wrong relationships can derail our destiny, so God will send you the right people at the right time to help you stay focused and propel you forward. Use the lessons those relationships teach you and move on. You do not have to be a product of a negative environment, nor feel bad about being set apart. In the words of Bishop T. D. Jakes, *'It does not matter where you start. It matters where you finish.'*

The Promise

▲▲▲▲▲▲▲▲▲▲▲▲

Events will happen in your life that will both scare and hurt you. Count it as an eye opener and a reminder of God's promises over your life. On Tuesday, November 12, 2018 I was en route to Columbia, SC from my college homecoming party. I was extremely tired, and I looked down for a split second to check my phone and to regroup. I looked up only to realize that I had rear-ended someone. I was terrified because just 30 minutes earlier I had a drink, and I was clearly in the wrong. I knew that if law enforcement came they would smell the alcohol on my breath. Even though I was not drunk, I just knew I was going to jail. Contrary to what I thought, the man I hit had no damages to his car and did not want to call law enforcement. Instead, he took my information and said that if he saw anything the following morning, he would call and we could handle it between us. I never heard from him and realized yet again that God had His hand on me - even in the midst of my sin. You would think that because I didn't go to jail or have to pay for damages to someone else's vehicle that it would be enough to say "*thank you, Lord*" and move on, but not for me. I was mad and really hurt because my car was totaled. It is crazy how the loss of material things can shake a man to his core, but I was over it. I was in a really bad space and I felt alone - like nobody was there for me. Bad choices caused me to destroy what I had worked hard and saved up to buy. Here is the clincher. I only had liability insurance so there was nothing my insurance company could do about my car. I had never been in this type of situation before so I was totally unprepared for what was next, but I quickly learned how difficult life was about to get.

When I went to the first auto repair shop for an assessment of the damages, they estimated $3700 plus tax - and told me to be prepared to pay more if they found internal damages. I had only paid $3500 for my car and had saved half of every check for years just to get enough money. There was no way I could pay that much to get it fixed. I reached out to numerous individuals for help, but found myself at a dead end each time. As if the car accident was not enough, for the first time in my life I had depleted my bank account. All of my gigs were being cancelled, one church fired me, I was behind in my schoolwork, and I was having major issues in my family. To top it off, I had lots of negative thoughts running around in my head. I found myself in the midst of a mental battle that I had to fight daily, but did not feel stable enough to win. I battled depression and allowed the situation to deter me from my purpose. At first I was in denial about the depression because I felt that if I spoke it, it would come into fruition. But, even without speaking it I found myself feeling like a dark cloud of sadness and misery was hovering over me. I lost my appetite, was restless, wanted to isolate myself from the world, and lost interest in everything that would lift my spirit. I had never been depressed like this before so it was an unfamiliar and uncomfortable place for me.

I gave up on everything, including God. I stopped tithing and I had no desire to go to church. In fact, I hated church. I was angry for no reason at all, and almost withdrew from college three times during my senior year. It felt like God had given up on me. Even when I tried my hardest to move on and take control of my life, I was mentally stuck in a permanent place of complacency. I can vividly remember sitting on the couch in my apartment with tears running down my face, my anxiety level on 1000, excruciating pain in my chest, and an unbearable headache. I started drinking to cope with my depression. One trip to the bar turned into multiple days at the bar, and when that got old I brought the liquor home and drank until I got tired. For the first time in my life, suicidal ideation crossed my mind and I did not see *one* reason to live. At least three times my girlfriend came home and found me just sitting in the dark, completely spaced out, drinking alcohol.

One of the days that she found me I remember having written a good-bye letter to my family. I planned to consume all the pills in my house and chase it down with liquor. Every time I picked up the pills I would look at myself in the mirror, and just break down in tears. I did not have the courage to do it because while I wanted to live, I just did not know how. I was smiling on the outside but deep inside I was broken, hurt, and confused. I would find myself thinking *"surely all of this can't come from a car wreck."* I did not understand it and while people would tell me what I needed to do and try to encourage me, it did not work. Frankly, I did not want it to work. I was tired and so out of it that I did not even realize how badly my health was declining. I was going back and forth to the hospital for chest pains, and initially charged it to drinking Red Bull, but it all turned out to be stress-related. I was 21 years old battling depression and was so stressed that my body started showing signs. This was not a part of the life I planned for myself and it surely was not how I wanted to die.

On November 15, 2018, after months of not praying, being spiritually frustrated and in a dark place, I plugged my headphones into my phone and searched Apple Music for a song similar to my situation - even though it was not what I needed. I was led to a song entitled *"The Promise"* by John Lakin and was pissed because I did not want to hear any gospel. But, I ended up playing that song on repeat with tears in my eyes until I fell asleep. I awakened feeling like God had literally snatched me right out of the pit and immediately restored me. That same day I texted the artist and told him that his song was the only thing keeping me sane, and had stopped me from throwing in the towel. His response was *"I love you bro. And I believe in you! Nobody who has ever done anything great... has done so without GREAT OPPOSITION."* That message opened my eyes to so much and at that point I began to apply the words of the song to my situation. I started declaring that indeed God made me a promise and if I only believed, things would get better for me! I was reassured that God's hand was still on me and my life. I grabbed hold of hope even in the midst of all the hell, and began to believe that His promise to me would not go unfulfilled. My pastor always says,"*If you are in a storm and wonder where God is, remember the instructor is always silent during the test.*"

Although I was really going through, had turned my back on God and the church, and felt like I almost lost my mind, that experience was necessary. It was indeed a test that taught me that even if I feel like God is delaying me, His promises are sure and cannot be denied. This had to be one of the scariest times of my life. I did not know if I was going to make it, but God knew. I was not strong enough and I gave up, but His strength was made perfect in my weakness. I now use this story when I am going through as a reminder that it is not as bad as it seems because I was once in a worse place.

Life Lesson:

God is not like man; He does not make promises He will not keep. As cliché as it may sound, if He said it then it will come pass. Sometimes a prayer life, scriptures, and church are the last things we want to hear or be reminded of when we are going through. But, those three essentials will quickly restore and encourage your heart and mind.

Plot Change

▲▲▲▲▲▲▲▲▲▲▲▲

Love has no age limit, color, or specified time when it will come; however, when true love shows up at your doorsteps, you will know it. You cannot fully embrace true love if you do not first know what it is or if you have the wrong perception about what it is.

For years I did not even love myself and that was the root of the issue when it came to showing love. Because of my exposure to domestic violence, manipulation, a traumatic experience with a member of my church, and the lack of a strong and authentic example of marriage - I had unaddressed issues that hindered me from being the man I should be. I exhibited some of the same behaviors I had seen modeled by men in my family and by my friends. As a result I subconsciously abused and mistreated women. While it was not physical, it still occurred. For years I believed that what I was doing was right. Deep down within I knew better and wanted to do better, but did not have the accountability or self-control to do so. I said I would be a better man, but my actions did not support my words.

To this day I do not know what came over me. I was legitimately uncomfortable with my behavior, and finally made a commitment to do the right thing. I made a vow to no longer be that type of man, whether subconsciously or on purpose. I had to do better. I wanted to get my head on straight and be the man that I wanted as a father. As soon as I made the change, it seems like God sent Danielle to me straight from His prized possession section of heaven. I knew that she was the one I wanted to marry when I saw her in church that Sunday. She became my friend and really took the time to learn who I was. Once she did that, she accepted my past and helped me embrace my future. When your partner understands your traumas, triggers, and past that is pivotal and it demonstrates authentic love.

For once in my life I had the same level of reciprocity and love, and since March 7, 2018, she has made my life so much better. I find myself thanking God for her daily. She supports me through everything and continuously epitomizes grace and strength. Together we have built the right foundation, and even in the tough moments there is still genuine honesty, trust, communication, happiness, and fun!

She did not come into my life alone, but brought two beautiful girls whom I love dearly. They are the most loving, funniest, animated, and caring girls ever. Because she had been a single mother for some time, I thought it would be pretty difficult for her to adjust to a consistent man in her and the kids' lives. But, it was not a major adjustment for any of us. We all just "clicked." It was so instantaneous that it was actually *scary*. The first time I met the girls, they ran to me and screamed my name as if they had known me all their lives. It was such a heartwarming moment.

I found myself constantly praying and asking God if I was making the right move in dating her. I did not want to build a relationship with her and the girls if she was not the one. I definitely did not want to add to the inconsistency and hurt that they had already experienced. God gave me my answer as I taught a Bible study lesson entitled "There's a Blessing in the Wait" on April 17, 2018. Psalm 27:14 was my base scripture and I selected a few other examples from the Bible where people had to wait on God, but the benefits they reaped were always worth the wait. A few days after I taught that, God told me that she was my blessing in the wait. That was all the confirmation I needed.

While it was never my intention to assume the role of stepfather at 20 or to date someone older than me, I am convinced daily that they are a part of my destiny. The girls and I have a bond that is inseparable, and I realized that I needed them just as much as they needed me. The girls give me an opportunity to be the father they need and the one I always wanted. I purpose to ensure that they are well taken care of, to be consistent, and to be whatever else they need me to be. I do not want them to experience the void in their hearts as I did. It still amazes me that I was so close to calling it quits with her because of the lack of support from my family and friends. But, I had to remember that I was not living for them, and that I had to make the decision that was best for me. Once I stopped trying to please everyone else, I began to see more and more that I had made the right choice for me. God showed me His love when He interrupted my life story with an unexpected plot change, and sent me Danielle Williams and her daughters.

Life Lesson:

True love still exists. Sometimes God will hold the blessing hostage until you are completely ready, so when it is released you will do right and cherish it. Don't rush into anything, take your time and wait on the right one for you. Pray about it, be specific about what you want, and trust God to send you exactly what you need. I am a witness that He will answer.

Strength and Restoration

▲▲▲▲▲▲▲▲▲▲▲▲▲

Given the life I have lived and everything I have been through so far, I was supposed to be a statistic and not even be alive. But God! Not only am I alive, I am content and have learned to appreciate my struggles. Everyday I learn a new lesson that reminds me why the endurance during my process was necessary. I am who I am today because of what I went through and as a result, I have been restored and have strength that sustains me daily. I consider my current place in life as evidence of God's unmerited favor. At 22 years old, God has given me everything I have ever asked Him to give me. While He often did not respond when I wanted Him to, He came through and that is what matters most. Besides, His timing is always prompt. When I reflect back on where I have come from, I am honestly in awe.

As I fore-stated, I am the first in my immediate family to graduate high school. I thought that was the best day of my life until May 2019 when I also became a first generation college graduate. It was on that day I realized the curse was broken and all I could think was, "*I really did it!*" On that same day I launched my nonprofit organization, "Choices," which was created to mentor and equip my community of young men to become purpose-driven, motivated, and successful despite their past or current circumstances. The goal of the organization is to do exactly what I want this book to do, motivate.

Coincidentally, as I am writing this book America is in the midst of major racial tension. We literally watched as a police officer, Derek Chauvin, murdered yet another unarmed Black man, George Floyd in the streets of Minneapolis, Minnesota. For 8 minutes and 46 seconds, Chauvin knelt on the neck of a handcuffed suspect being arrested for using counterfeit money until the blood flow to his brain was cut off. We watched as two additional officers knelt on his back, cutting off air to his lungs as he repeatedly said, '*I can't breathe.*' We watched him call out for his deceased mother right before his body went limp. As a result, protests, rallies, and looting have taken over cities across the US and the world. Blacks, whites and others have come together in unity to declare that it is time for change. It is clear that people are hurt, tired, and furious.

Unfortunately, this is nothing new. Black men have for ages experienced racial profiling, been harassed by police, been given unjust sentences, jailed for crimes that they did not commit, and killed. Black men fear for their lives when encountering police, and mothers and fathers take great care to instruct their sons (and daughters) how to engage with police just to try and keep them alive. It is not new, we simply see more given the prevalence of camera phones that allow almost everyone to record these interactions. While I had no way of knowing, God did - and this book comes at a most opportune time - to encourage Black men and remind us that despite our challenges, we can make it.

The plight of Black men in America - and subsequently my hometown - is at the core of my decision to take "CHOICES" back to my hometown. We must educate and influence as many young men as possible to pursue a path that will lead to positive life outcomes. To pursue a path that will minimize their interaction with police. For me, it starts with my brother. It would be selfish and disheartening of me to help other young men and leave my brother behind. He saw abuse and the doggish mentality of men in our family much longer than even I did. So, I will work tirelessly to help him see that he has choices, and that his life matters. I want to reach back and help as many young men as possible climb the ladder of success with the official launch of CHOICES in the fall of 2021. Having someone consistently push you to greatness helps you become the best version of yourself. In the words of Dr. Martin Luther King Jr, *"If I can help somebody as I pass along, if I can cheer somebody with a word or song, if I can show somebody he's traveling wrong, then my living will not be in vain."*

Two months after graduation and birthing my organization, I started a job with the state as a Department of Social Services (DSS) employee. All I could say was *"Thank you Jesus"* because God was orchestrating everything for me. I could literally see things falling into place just as He promised. I also currently serve as a full-time music director at a local church and am in the process of launching a lawn care business. A wise man once told me, *"no man became wealthy and successful by just doing one thing."* With that in mind, I will continue to add streams of income so I can take care of my family and invest in my community.

In addition to those successes, it was a dream come true on February 28, 2020 when I received my acceptance letter from Gupton-Jones School of Mortuary Science. If I do not accomplish anything else in this life, I want to get that under my belt. Once I graduate and am licensed, I plan to become the Founder and Chief Operating Officer of Rutledge Funeral Home and Crematory. I am determined to use what my mentors at Wilds invested in me, coupled with what I learn from Gupton-Jones, to effectively run a business that will serve families with dignity, professionalism, and love. The passion I have to help those with whom I come in contact will continue to be exhibited through my funeral home. I have already assembled my team and scouted out potential locations for my launch. Be sure you stay tuned for my grand opening, then watch us become a flourishing and dependable business worldwide.

Jonathan McReynolds sings a song entitled "*God is Good*," and if I had to pick a song to describe my life right now that would be my pick. Not to be super deep or "churchy," but every struggle, mishap, and downfall that I have experienced in life thus far has shaped me into a better and stronger man. They have simply proven that God is good. I am far from perfect. I still have so many things to work on and goals to accomplish; nevertheless, I wanted to write this book right where I am in life currently to show the world that no matter the background from which one started, he can still make it. We have options and the ultimate choice is ours. The journey may be arduous, but it is necessary. It will sometimes become stressful, and the obstacles you encounter will make it seem like you will not make it. But I am living, breathing proof that there is sunshine at the end of the storm.

Better is an accessible lifestyle free to all who are willing to pursue it. Life can sometimes blind us to it, yet it is always present. Let me be crystal clear so you can set yourself up for success. You will not reach your goals without enduring some hardships. My life's story is evidence of that. But, let me also encourage you with these four words, *"Trouble doesn't last always."* That is churchy, I know, so let me put it this way. You have options. I cannot beat around the bush with you. You cannot lose focus and become stagnated. It is easier said than done I know, but I realized during my depression that if I at least tried, God would do the rest. It doesn't matter where you come from - nor your race, your mistakes, your inconsistencies, or your circumstances. Your life has purpose and you can make it.

Life Lesson:

"Success in life comes when you simply refuse to give up, with goals so strong that obstacles, failure, and loss only act as motivation."

Guidance for the Journey

▲▲▲▲▲▲▲▲▲▲▲▲

As I stated in the beginning of this book, life is filled with many changes and obstacles but it is imperative that we realize it is simply a part of the journey. While we all bring some stuff on ourselves, there are some tests and trials assigned to our lives for our development. We must go through those assignments as good soldiers, knowing that we will make it. We sometimes forget that God has equipped us with everything we need to be overcomers, that we literally have everything at our fingertips. If we seek Him and heed the counsel He provides, we will be just fine.

With that in mind, I believe it is both beneficial as well as fitting to close this book offering you encouragement and tips to help you along the way. In this chapter I will elaborate on some tools that have helped me in my journey to success. I hope they will do the same for you. I realized a few years ago that I can lead you to water, but it is your choice whether to drink or not. In other words, I can give you everything I have, but it is your job to heed the advice.

Prayer

Prayer gives us a direct line of communication with the Father, and is the only conversation where we are guaranteed a response. Effective, fervent prayer is powerful. Our moments of vulnerability are not the time to rely on friends or family, but definitely the time to turn to God.

Prayer is a lifestyle and should not be something that we only pull out when we *need* it. We must be consistent and give God 10 times more than the time we spend roaming social media. I know that prayer saved my life numerous times.

Acceptance

Learning to accept the things we cannot change can be one of the most trying experiences. There are some things that we will seemingly never get past, but if we can learn to just embrace the fact that it is what it is and glean the lessons, we will ultimately find peace. That is one of the greatest gifts we can give to ourselves.

Endurance

With every journey we must have endurance - the ability to wait on something you want or need. You may have to be in the waiting room a long time, and you will likely become a little weary. There will be times when you will even want to quit and throw in the towel, but I encourage you to stay in the fight. If you leave too soon, you will run the risk of delaying your blessing or obtaining a counterfeit blessing prematurely. Trust me, you do not want either one. The true blessing of God is well worth the wait!

Trust the process

When it feels like life is falling apart right before our eyes, we must stay positive - even in the things we speak. We must hold on to our faith in the way-making, unwavering God and trust both the process and His timing. In fact, "Trust the Process" was almost the title of this book because, in essence, that is what I learned to do. Amidst all the adversity I faced, my process made me the man I am today. Had I not trusted the process through the stress of it all, I am not sure where I would be. 1 Peter 5:10 states, "*And after you have suffered a little while, the God of all grace, who has called you to His eternal glory in Christ, will Himself restore, confirm, strengthen, and establish you.*" The process helps to renew our faith, establish and strengthen us. God knew that we would get weak and face moments of affliction, so He promised us that if we would just withstand our current situation and have faith in Him, He would give us restoration. Whatever it takes, trust your process because the benefits, both spiritual and physical, outweigh the pain of the process.

Self-care

This is something that I cannot stress enough - especially for men. We are often faced with so much that we do not take the time to care for ourselves. We hide our true feelings and emotions because we do not want to be deemed weak or "less of man," but in doing so we jeopardize our mental health. So we must be intentional about making time for self-care. When you do so, it encourages a healthy relationship with yourself.

When we pay attention to our well-being, we are reinvigorating ourselves and ensuring that we are the best version of ourselves for the people around us. Know who you are and when you need to step away for rejuvenation. Your body will always give you warnings so do not ignore them. By practicing good self-care you show others that your life matters, and that you are committed to preserving yourself.

Understanding these topics and their importance is vital. The key to full success requires both understanding and action. Continue to make your goals, dreams, and visions attainable. Do not stop grinding! Do not allow anyone or anything to stop you from pursuing success. Why? I am so glad you asked. If you can dream it, you can attain it. You just have to keep your hope alive! Your dreams need grit, boldness, stamina, and resilience to survive. And yes, there is so much more to this thing called my *life*, but I chose to share what I thought would be some transparent and relatable portions as a reminder that with the right choices, you too can make it. Believing that is the first step to making it a reality.

The Author

Nazaire Rutledge is a musician, author, and mentor from Georgetown, SC. He is a graduate of Claflin University and the founder of a non-profit organization for young men called CHOICES. This purpose-driven, motivated, and successful man is determined to succeed no matter what comes his way. His favorite quote is, *"Success in life comes*

when you simply refuse to give up, with goals so strong that obstacles, failure, and loss only act as motivation."

For more information and booking please contact us at choices957@gmail.com.